The Extraordinarily Ordinary Life of

Cassandra Jones

Southwest Cougars Year 1

Southwest Cougars Year 1: Age 12

Episode 1: Growing Girls
The Extraordinarily Ordinary Life of Cassandra Jones

Tamara Hart Heiner

print edition
copyright 2017 Tamara Hart Heiner
cover art by Tamara Hart Heiner

Also by Tamara Hart Heiner:
Perilous (WiDo Publishing 2010)
Altercation (WiDo Publishing 2012)
Deliverer (Tamark Books 2014)
Priceless (WiDo Publishing 2016)

Goddess of Fate:
Inevitable (Tamark Books 2013)
Entranced (Tamark Books 2017)

Kellam High:
Lay Me Down (Tamark Books 2016)
Reaching Kylee (Tamark Books 2016)

The Extraordinarily Ordinary Life of Cassandra Jones:
Walker Wildcats Year 1 (Tamark Books 2016)
Walker Wildcats Year 2 (Tamark Books 2016)

Tornado Warning (Dancing Lemur Press 2014)

Table of Contents

Episode 1: Growing Girl

Chapter One
Andrea's Birthday

"I can't believe we're about to start junior high," Cassandra Jones said, watching as her best friend Andrea pulled out a tray of different colored nail polishes.

The two girls sat in Andrea's bedroom, both perched on the bed with Andrea's white coverlet. Everything in Andrea's room was white, and Cassie always felt like she'd entered a serene fairy land when she came over. Nothing like the mad chaos that existed at her house, between her three siblings, their dog, and one cat. Their cat had a kitten a few years ago, but Mrs. Jones gave it away to another family and fixed the cat so it would never have another kitten.

"I know," Andrea said, pulling Cassie back to the conversation as she selected a bright red polish. Like Cassie, she wore glasses and kept her hair long. But hers was a wavy honey-brown with a hint of red, while Cassie's was dark, dark brown and very straight. "What do you think it will be like?"

Cassie shook her head, a nervous sensation bubbling in her stomach. She hated to admit how it frightened her, moving from elementary school to junior high. She chose a hot pink nail polish. She uncapped it and dragged the brush from the bottom of her nail bed to the top, glad she didn't bite her nails anymore. "I hope we have classes together."

"That's the scary part, right?" Andrea sighed. "We have no idea what classes we'll have."

Cassie squirmed. Just two years ago her family had moved to Arkansas from Texas, and it had taken this long for her to feel she had a place, a good group of friends. It hadn't been easy to make them. What would happen if she and Andrea didn't have classes together? Would she have classes with anyone she knew?

As if reading her mind, Andrea glanced at her and winked. "Maybe you'll have classes with Miles."

Miles. Cassie's lips curved upward as his face, complete with his friendly smile, appeared in her mind. A warmth flowed through her chest. Only to Andrea had she ever admitted her crush on their classmate. Miles, of course, had no idea, and Cassie never intended to tell him.

"Isn't your birthday party in a week?" Cassie asked, changing the subject before Andrea could pry her more. Andrea always urged her to tell Miles her feelings, but the thought terrified her.

"Yes, but I'm not having a slumber party. It's just for a few hours." Andrea capped the nail polish and blew across her fingers. "I'll text you the date."

"Great," Cassie said with a giggle. She and Andrea had both gotten phones after they graduated elementary school, and texting back and forth was enormous fun. Cassie didn't actually like to talk on it very much, though Andrea did. "I have soccer camp in a few weeks, and church camp a week after that, so as long as it's before then, we should be fine."

"I thought you decided you didn't like soccer?"

Cassie leaned back, waving her newly-polished nails to dry them. "I do like soccer. I'm just really bad at it." And she hated running, and the other kids on her team, especially Connor Lane, always made fun of her. "Hopefully a week of soccer camp will help me improve."

"Well, my party is next week. So you should be fine. But guess what!" Andrea pushed upward against the bed, her eyes lighting up with excitement. She grabbed Cassie's hands, careful to avoid her nails, and pumped them excitedly.

"What, what?" Cassie said, growing excited as well.

"Kitty's coming!"

For a moment Cassie just blinked at her, and then her memory jolted. She remembered Andrea talking about her old best friend Kitty, the one who moved away in the middle of fifth grade. Cassie had seen her once or twice, but she'd been in the other classroom, so they didn't know each other. But now a flash of jealousy rippled through her. If Kitty hadn't moved, would Kitty and Andrea still be best friends?

"Oh, that's nice," Cassie said, trying to hide her insecurities.

"I know you two will just love each other. You'll get along so great." Andrea squeezed Cassie's hands, the smile on her lips threatening to split her face.

"I'm sure," Cassie said, her heart starting to pound at the thought of spending time with Kitty. She pictured the other girl as she remembered her in her mind's eye: much taller than Cassie, skinny, with short brown hair. Glancing toward the mirror, Cassie frowned at her reflection. Large pink glasses framed her brown eyes, and the roundness to her face only emphasized her shortness. Her hands pulled away from Andrea and went down to squeeze the pudge that had gradually built up around her waist over the past year. Her frown deepened.

It's fine, she told herself. *Andrea's your best friend.* And yet, she couldn't shake the feeling that this was an unwanted complication.

Friday morning, the day of Andrea's birthday party, Cassie rushed through the required assignments her mom had given her so she could go to the party. She had just finished folding laundry and putting it away in the bedroom she shared with her sister Emily when she got a text from Andrea.

Can you come early to my birthday party and help set up?

Cassie lifted one eyebrow in surprise. The party started in just four hours. Her mom might not appreciate the late notice.

Cassie wandered out into the hallway, nearly tripping over her youngest brother and sister, Scott and Annette, as they built a large track out of wooden blocks. "Guys," she growled at them, but they merely glanced at her and then looked away, uninterested in her annoyance.

"Mom?" The door was open to her parents' bedroom, so she stepped in and sat across from her mom on the bed.

Mrs. Jones looked up from the envelopes she was stamping. "Yes, Cassie?"

"Andrea wants to know if I can come early and help set up for her birthday party."

"What time does she want you there?" Mrs. Jones put a stamp on another envelope and placed it in the stamped pile.

"I don't know."

"Tell her I can drop you off at noon."

That was an hour before the party started. Should be plenty of time. Cassie's thumbs flew over the keypad as she texted, *I'll be there at noon.*

Great! Thank you! came Andrea's response.

Cassie hesitated, but she had to know. Quickly she typed out, *Is Kitty there?*

Not yet, Andrea said. *She'll get here when everyone else does.*

Some of the tightness went out of Cassie's chest. Andrea might be glad that Kitty was coming, but Cassie was still her best friend.

"This is the last year we'll be playing 'Pin the Tail on the Donkey,'" Andrea said as she and Cassie spread the plastic sheet across the wall.

"Why?" Cassie asked.

"Because we're too old for it." One of Andrea's eyebrows lifted. "We're going into the seventh grade. Next year we'll all be thirteen. No one will want to play this baby game."

"Hmm." Cassie nodded, though she wasn't sure it would be true. Could they all really change so much in one year?

Andrea let out a little giggle. "Remember your twelfth birthday, when your dog threw up on you? Hilarious."

Cassie remembered. Her face burned, and she was glad that her dark complexion would hide the blush. "Not really his fault. He's epileptic."

"Yeah, but still—and right before people started coming over!"

Andrea kept giggling, but Cassie tried not to think about the incident. Her birthdays lately hadn't gone all that well. This year she planned to forgo a party altogether. "Hopefully your party goes better than mine."

The doorbell rang, and Andrea swiveled around, dropping the pile of donkey tails onto the bookshelf. "Kitty!"

She raced for the door. Cassie lagged behind uncertainly, not sure of her role here.

Andrea threw open the front door. "Kitty!"

"Andy!" Kitty, even taller than when Cassie had seen her in fifth grade, squealed just as loudly as Andrea. Then they threw their arms around each other and swayed in a giant hug.

Cassie wrinkled her nose. *Andy?* Since when?

Since before Cassie, she guessed.

Andrea pulled out of the embrace first. "Kitty, do you know Cassie? She was in Ms.

9

Dawson's class."

"Hi." Kitty smiled and waved, revealing braces with multicolored bands on them. She no longer wore glasses, either, leaving a clear line of sight to her light brown eyes.

"Hi," Cassie replied. Feeling awkward, she added, "Glad you could come."

"Come on, I want to show you a few things in my room," Andrea said, taking Kitty's hand. "Cassie, can you finish setting out the paper plates and cups?"

"You don't want me to come with you?" Cassie said, surprised at the dismissal.

Andrea brushed her off. "You were just in here. Kitty hasn't seen my room in almost two years."

Cassie forced a smile. "Of course. It's your birthday. I'll do whatever you need."

Andrea's mom joined Cassie in the kitchen, and they finished setting out the paper plates and cups. Even from here Cassie could hear Andrea and Kitty laughing and talking excitedly in the bedroom. Cassie's chest tightened.

The doorbell rang, and Mrs. Wall yelled, "Andrea! Your guests are arriving!"

"Coming!" Andrea shouted back.

A steady stream of kids showed up for the next several minutes, and Andrea spent all her time greeting them and directing them to Cassie, who seated them in the living room. Then they played musical chairs, and Andrea paid no more attention to Kitty than she did to all her friends. By the time they got to Pin the Tail on the Donkey, Cassie had relaxed. Kitty was only here for a few hours, after all.

"Presents!" Mrs. Wall shouted, bringing out the large stack that had collected by the front door. "Andrea, sit in the middle of the floor."

Andrea obliged, finding a spot facing everyone on the two couches.

Cassie spotted her present right away. Her mom had placed the straw hat in a hatbox and then wrapped it in shiny turquoise paper. A big green bow sat on top. Cassie just knew Andrea would love it.

"That one's mine," Kitty said, pointing to a massive pink box. "Open it first, please!"

Cassie frowned at Kitty. How dare she steal the show? Then she swiveled back to Andrea, waiting to see what she would say.

"Okay," Andrea laughed. She picked up the present and slowly peeled back the paper. Then she gasped. "Oh, wow."

Cassie craned her head, trying to see what it was. She needn't have bothered. Andrea undid the box and pulled out a large, light-pink crystal unicorn. The back legs were suspended on a pedestal while the front legs kicked up and out, as if the animal were about to take a flying leap.

Cassie's heart clenched. It was beautiful. Feminine and grown-up and expensive. Suddenly, she wanted to retrieve her hatbox and run from the room.

"Oh, Kitty!" Andrea gasped. "I love it!"

Cassie gritted her teeth while the two girls hugged—again. She wove her fingers together and watched as Andrea opened the other presents, finally getting to Cassie's.

"And this one's yours, of course," she said, flashing Cassie a smile. "I saved the best for last."

The words didn't comfort Cassie; instead, she only felt more embarrassed by her gift. "Don't get too excited. It's pretty lame." Especially compared to Kitty's.

"Never," Andrea admonished. She pulled up the bow, then peeled back the wrapping paper. Curiosity showed on her face as she lifted the lid to the box.

"This is beautiful!" she exclaimed, pulling out the straw hat, complete with flowers on the brim and a ribbon to tie it under her neck. "Thank you, Cassie!"

Cassie forced herself to smile while Andrea hugged her, but she felt like she was being patronized. The hat had looked so cute in the antique shop. Now, next to the other gifts Andrea had received, it looked like something for a little girl.

When the party ended, the guests began to clear out, except for Cassie and Kitty. Andrea thanked everyone as they left. Cassie sat stiffly on the couch, wondering when Kitty's mom would show up.

"Where's your mom, Cassie?" Kitty asked from the other end of the couch, as if thinking the same thing.

"Oh, I'm staying late," Cassie said, glad Andrea had asked her to stay after the party as well. "Andrea asked me to stay over after."

Kitty looked surprised. "I didn't know that."

"What about you?" Cassie glanced toward the door, where Andrea bade goodbye to the last guest. "Where's your mom?"

"I'm spending the weekend here. With Andrea."

A knot tightened in Cassie's stomach. Andrea had failed to mention that. "That will be so great. A chance for you two to catch up." *Without me.* Cassie pictured them forming a new, tighter bond than ever, replete with inside jokes and personal references that Cassie would never understand.

"Yeah. My parents are looking at houses. We might move back here."

The knot doubled up on itself. "Nice," Cassie said through gritted teeth.

Andrea rejoined them on the couch and

sighed. "I couldn't have asked for a better birthday! I'm so glad you both were here and could help so much!"

"It was nothing," Cassie said, inexplicably close to tears.

Andrea picked up the hat Cassie had given her and placed it on her head. "How do I look?" She smiled and posed, batting her eyelashes at Cassie.

"Lovely, dah-ling," Cassie said, adopting a fake British accent. "I ah-dore you in that hat."

"I have to see." Andrea jumped up and ran to the bathroom. Kitty followed, and Cassie trooped along behind. Next to Kitty's tall, slender frame, all she wanted was to be taller and skinnier.

Giggling, Andrea took the hat off and pushed up on her hair. "It needs to be bigger. Hair spray, Cassie."

After more slumber parties over here than Cassie could count, she knew which cupboard had the hair spray. She handed it over to Andrea, who finished ratting her hair and then solidified it with the spray.

"Your turn, Cassie. Make it big."

Cassie held the can of spray and stared at her thick, straight hair. What could she possibly do with it? "I don't know how."

"I'll do it." Kitty took the hair spray and shoved almost all of her short golden hair to the side of her head. Then she sprayed it, waving the can back and forth as she pelted the hair with tiny droplets. When she finished, part of it fell into her face in a desperate attempt to return to its rightful place. She looked sexy and modern.

"Let me try." Cassie took the hair spray and swept her hair over to the side. Squinting her eyes, she held the spray tip down and coated her hair with the sticky wetness. Most of it held, only a small amount falling out of formation to form a wave across her forehead. She liked the look.

"We look so grown up," Andrea said, pulling out a container of make-up. "Now to finish it."

Kitty chuckled. "You've always thought yourself the make-up artist."

"Yeah," Cassie joined in, laughing. "And my mom makes me take it all off as soon as I get home."

Kitty looked at her, and they laughed together. Something loosened in Cassie's chest. Maybe there didn't have to be a competition between them.

Then she remembered that Kitty was spending the night. No, the sooner Kitty left again, the better.

Chapter Two
Soccer Camp

"I'm so excited for soccer camp," Cassie's younger sister Emily said. She quickly piled clothing into the suitcase spread wide open on her bed. "Isn't it great? Our coaches will all be professional soccer players from the university."

Cassie wasn't sure a student could be a professional soccer player, but she didn't correct her sister. Instead she stood by her dresser, eyes glazing over as she watched Emily.

Emily closed her suitcase and zipped it up, then shoved her long light brown hair out of her face. She looked at Cassie. "Aren't you going to pack?"

Cassie sighed and opened up a drawer, unmotivated in spite of the fact that they would leave for camp tomorrow after church. She'd asked for this. She'd begged her parents to let her play soccer, and they'd finally agreed, signing her and Emily up for it. The end result? She sucked at it. And instead of each practice getting easier, it only got harder.

"What are you afraid of?" Emily asked, as if reading her mind. "I thought you loved soccer."

"I do." Cassie dumped a pair of pajamas in her own suitcase. "But I don't think it loves me."

Emily giggled at that. "Well, after this week, I'm sure you'll be great at it."

Cassie appreciated her sister's vote of confidence, but she had her doubts.

When church ended on Sunday, Mr. Jones drove the two younger kids, Scott and Annette, home while Mrs. Jones drove the girls to the University of Arkansas in Fayetteville, just twenty minutes away. They pulled into a parking lot at the multi-leveled dorms. Cassie watched the other kids unloading their suitcases from the cars. Most of the girls were thick but muscular, with long hair trapped in ponytail holders and athletic shorts on. She looked down at her skirt and wished she'd had time to change.

"We need some cool shorts like that," Emily said.

"You want some?" Mrs. Jones asked.

"They're kind of nice," Emily said, a little sheepishly.

"Well, I have a surprise for you," Mrs. Jones said. "Let's check the trunk."

Intrigued, Cassie undid her seatbelt and followed her sister to the back of the van. Mrs. Jones popped it open, and next to the two suitcases was a large paper bag.

"Open it," her mother said.

Emily did, and she gasped as she pulled out a pair of bright blue shorts with a lime-green cuff. "These are awesome!"

Eagerly, Cassie pulled out another pair, this one purple with the same lime-green cuff. "I love them! Where did you get them?"

Mrs. Jones beamed at them. "Since Scott and Annette want to play soccer also, your dad's been searching everywhere for a good place to get your soccer supplies. He realized there just isn't one. So—he's going to start one."

Cassie's eyes widened. Her dad loved to take on new projects. The last one he'd done was a band at her elementary school. "Wow! That will be fun."

Mrs. Jones' smile weakened slightly. "Fun— and expensive and time-consuming."

Definitely time-consuming. "But he has a job," Cassie said. "How will he fit it in?"

Her mom's smile disappeared completely. "He's quitting his job. This is a venture he wants to embark on, and I'm supporting him."

Sounded great to Cassie. She loved how her dad was taking this leap of faith to pursue his dream.

"We'll need you girls to help out a bit in the store sometimes," Mrs. Jones went on.

"Like a job?" Cassie said, growing more

excited.

"A very low-paying one, yes," Mrs. Jones said.

It had to be more than her measly allowance. Cassie picked up her suitcase, a little more pep to her step as she walked toward the dormitory.

A woman with short brown hair and a whistle around her neck greeted them in the foyer. She wore no make up, and her shirt stretched tight across her shoulders. The muscles on her arms flexed as she lifted her pencil. "Names?" she said, looking over her clipboard.

"Cassandra and Emily Jones," Mrs. Jones said, resting a hand on each girl's shoulder.

"Okay, you're rooming together on the second floor. Just take the elevator there—" she pointed behind her— "and go right. You'll see your names on the door. You'll be rooming with two other girls. Oh, and no elevators after today. We take the stairs." She winked at both girls.

They shuffled into the elevator, and as the

doors closed, Emily leaned over and whispered, "That's what a real soccer player looks like."

Cassie nodded. Athletic. There was no other way to describe the woman. She looked down at the roll of skin around her belly, and the first word that came to mind was "portly."

"Hi," a girl with very curly brown hair and braces said when the girls dragged their suitcases into their room. She sat on the bottom bunk of one of the two bunk beds, her phone in her hands. "I'm Olivia."

"Cassie," Cassie said, choosing the bottom bunk of the bed closest to the door.

"I'm Emily."

"Our other roommate is Tara, but she hasn't come yet," Olivia said.

Cassie nodded. She turned to her mom with a big smile, suddenly eager to be on their own. "We got it from here, Mom."

"I guess it's time I headed home anyway," Mrs. Jones said. "Good luck, girls! We'll see you at the big game on Friday."

"Right," Emily said, already unloading her

things on the top bunk. "I forgot we'd be playing for you."

"Yeah, all week we'll work on our skills. Isn't it cool that the actual Lady Razorback soccer players will be coaching us?" Olivia beamed.

"Bye, girls." Mrs. Jones hugged them both, then, with a final wave, she walked out.

Cassie barely glanced at her retreating back, focusing instead on arranging her things in the little space around her bed.

"Where are you from?" Olivia asked.

"Springdale," Cassie said. "You?"

"Where's that? I'm from Conway. It's about three hours from here."

"Oh. Springdale's only twenty minutes away."

"Nice! So do you go to a lot of the Razorback games?"

Olivia looked so eager, almost hungry in expectation, that Cassie felt bad admitting they weren't Razorback fans. "No."

Olivia leaned back on her bottom bunk, disappointment passing over her features. "I want to be one of the Lady Razorbacks one day. I've been playing soccer for five years. Next year I'm joining a competitive team."

"Really?" Cassie gave Olivia another look. "How old are you?"

"Eleven."

Cassie frowned. "So you're only going into sixth grade?"

"Yep. You?"

Cassie pointed at herself and said, "Seventh." Then she gestured to Emily and said, "Fifth."

"We've only been playing for a few months," Emily said.

"You must really like it to be coming to camp already."

"We hope to improve," Cassie said. "Have you come to camp before?"

"Yeah. This is my second year. I started coming as soon as I was old enough."

"What's your favorite part about camp?" Cassie asked. She put her suitcase under the bed, changing her mind about unpacking.

"The ice cream," Olivia said immediately.

"We eat at a buffet in the cafeteria, and they have ice cream. Not the soft-serve kind, but the kind you have to scoop out. I have it with every meal."

"Every meal?" Emily echoed, her eyes widening.

"Yep." Olivia smiled and bobbed her head up and down.

Cassie pressed a hand to her stomach. She doubted she needed an ice cream with every meal.

"What else do you like?" Emily asked.

"Well, the soccer is fun, but it's grueling. Like super hard. Like you want to fall-on-the-grass-and-drown-in-your-water-bottle hard. But the final game is so worth it. They break us up into two teams and we play each other. No matter who wins, we all feel like winners. Because after five days with each other, we're one unit, you know?"

Cassie nodded, though she didn't know. She didn't really get along with anyone on her current soccer team. Some of the girls were friendly, but she knew no one really valued her. She hated running, and her foot missed the ball more often than it connected with it.

The more she thought about it, the more she really didn't know why she was here.

"But also Thursday night, before our last game, there's a talent show."

Her ears perked up again. "Talent show?" she asked. "Like who dribbles the best or who can pass the ball with the most control?"

Olivia laughed. "No, it doesn't have to be soccer related at all. Some people sing, play the piano, or tell jokes. Whatever."

"Cassie sings opera," Emily said.

"Ew, opera?" Olivia wrinkled her nose. "Nobody likes opera."

"No, really," Emily said. "It's fun. Sing something, Cass."

Cassie hesitated, then belted out the first two lines from a popular musical in full-on opera style.

"Ahh!" Olivia and Emily burst out laughing, holding their sides with mirth.

"Keep going!" Olivia shrieked. "Do some more!"

Grinning, Cassie obliged, singing the rest of the song like a star performer.

Monday morning, the camp director, Carol, came around and knocked on all the bedroom doors.

"Socks and shinguards on, girls!" she shouted as she walked down the hall. "Ten minutes to eat your breakfast, and then meet me in the foyer!"

Cassie peeked one eye out from under her arm while Olivia groaned.

"We stayed up way too late last night," Olivia said.

"Yeah," Emily agreed from the top bunk, a yawn stifling her words.

Tara had come in later in the evening, after dinner, but the four girls had hit it off. They'd stayed up talking, and Cassie was pleased that the subject of soccer wasn't brought up at all. Now Tara lifted her blond head off the pillow just enough for Cassie to see it bob above the top bunk frame.

"Seven a.m.!" Tara groaned. "What are they

doing to us?"

"It's like this every day," Olivia said. She'd already slipped on a soccer jersey and shorts, and now she pulled on her socks. "She's not kidding, either. We better run to breakfast or we won't get any."

Cassie hurriedly pulled on her t-shirt and new shorts, then her shinguards and knee-high socks. The four girls rushed out of the dorm room and down the stairs to the cafeteria on the first floor. Cassie grabbed a muffin and a banana and joined the group of girls in the foyer.

"The soccer field is just a few hundred meters away," Carol was saying. "And the best time of the day to be out there playing is right now, before it gets too hot. So put on your jogging hat and let's go!"

Cassie hadn't even eaten yet! She shoved half the muffin in her mouth and tossed the other half at a trashcan. The banana she held gently in one hand as the girls headed out the door, breaking into an easy jog.

Although Cassie started the run next to

Emily, in about the middle of the group, between the chewing and swallowing and the actual running, she had to slow down. Before she knew it, she was at the back of the group. How much farther to the soccer fields? She squinted and looked down the sidewalk where they ran, two dozen other girls keeping pace in front of her. Brick buildings banked the concrete on one side, the road on the other. She didn't see any sign of a soccer field.

Her side began to cramp, and Cassie came to a halt. It would be easier to finish her food first and then run. She walked along behind, unpeeling her banana and keeping her eyes open for the fields. The pack of girls got farther and farther ahead. She ate her banana as quickly as she could, glancing around for a trashcan before shrugging and tossing the peel in the grass. She figured it would decompose.

When she looked up again, her heart gave a little leap. The camp of girls was about the turn the corner without her. Crapola! She'd never live it down if she showed up ten

minutes after everyone else. Adrenaline surging her onward, Cassie broke into a jog again. The cramp in her side flared up even worse, and she pressed a hand to it, leaning heavily to one side with each step downward. Her breathing came in short, raspy gasps.

She turned the corner and saw the soccer field. Bleachers surrounded it on two sides, and red water coolers with plastic cups on top of them sat on top of tables nestled in the bright green grass.

Almost there! She told herself. She wanted

to stop running. So badly.

Emily lifted her head and saw her, and her face lit up. "Cassie!" she called. "What happened to you?"

Almost as one, all the other girls turned to look at her. Some wore expressions of surprise, and others confusion. The confusion turned to derision, and a few girls huddled their heads together and whispered.

"Nothing happened to me," Cassie snapped, annoyed her sister had pointed her out. She stopped by one of the water coolers and poured a cup of water. "I had to stop a few times."

Carol's whistle blew. "All right, ladies! Every time we come to the fields, that's how we'll get here. When we head home after practice, we'll go the same way. By the end of the week, you'll be running a mile without breaking a sweat."

Cassie broke out in a sweat just hearing those words. Was this lady crazy? No way was she doing all that running.

Carol's eyes focused on another part of the

field, and she smiled. Cassie followed her gaze as five tall, muscular young women walked onto the field, dressed in red and white shorts and jerseys, their hair tied back with red ribbons.

"And look!" Carol said. "Our Lady Razorbacks are here! I'll number you off into three groups. Each group will have two instructors." She counted them off, and Cassie broke off to join the group she was assigned to.

Carol called out, "We'll regroup in half an hour. Listen to your instructors, ladies!"

"Razorbacks!" shouted the instructors in the red and white jerseys. All of the campers looked at them, and Carol laughed before marching away.

So these were the Lady Razorbacks. Cassie scrutinized them. What was it about them that Olivia so admired?

It only took about two minutes of practice to figure it out.

"Hi, I'm Laine," the brunette with freckles across her nose said. "I'm a sophomore at the

U of A, and this is my second year on the team."

"And I'm Rishika," the other girl said, a slight accent in her words. "I came on a soccer scholarship. This is my first year. If you play soccer really well in high school, you can earn a scholarship too."

"How many of you want to go to the U of A?" Laine asked.

Several of the girls cheered, waving their arms. Cassie didn't. She wanted to go to the same school her father had gone to.

"Fantastic! And how many of you want to play for the Lady Razorbacks?"

The cheers turned into screams, loud, excited, delirious screams.

"Then let's get on it, ladies!"

"Razorbacks!" Rishika shouted.

Laine tossed everyone a ball, and she and Rishika demonstrated how to steal the ball, make a feint, and pass the ball to a teammate in the back.

"Now everyone grab a partner and try these passes!" Laine said.

Passing wasn't too hard. Cassie paired up with Nikki, a redhead from West Fork who was also going into seventh grade.

"Hey, you've got good footwork," Nikki said.

"Thanks," Cassie said, feeling a bit more confident.

"You girls are doing good," Rishika said, walking around and watching everyone. "Looks like you know how to control the ball."

They went through the drills a few more times and then took a water break.

"Time for a scrimmage," Carol said, gathering the girls back together into one group. "All of you—against me and the Ladies."

"Razorbacks!" the Lady Razorbacks shouted. This time a few of the campers said it with them.

"Oh, easy!" someone said, and the campers laughed and jeered.

"We'll see how easy this is," Carol scoffed. "Olivia, you're team captain. I want three on offense, two on defense, and one in the goal. Decide who's playing first."

Olivia turned around. "Okay, who wants to play what?"

Cassie opened her mouth to claim defense, but two girls beat her to it. Emily and another girl claimed offense, and Olivia looked at Cassie.

"Cassie, do you want to play offense also?"

Cassie shook her head. "No, I do best on defense."

"What about goalie?"

"No way." It took a certain kind of player to be goalie, and it sure wasn't Cassie.

"I'll play goalie," another, much bigger, girl said.

"Thanks," Olivia said. "What's your name?"

"Gretchen."

"Okay, Gretchen's in goal." Olivia turned back to Cassie. "Want to try offense today, Cass?"

Cassie wanted to say no. But the way Olivia said her name, as if they were friends—

"Okay."

"Great. Come on, everyone, let's scrimmage!"

Emily stepped up to the starting line, standing in the middle of the field. Cassie took the spot to her left. Even though she'd been playing soccer for a few months, she so rarely played striker that she wasn't quite sure what would happen next. The whistle blew, and Emily passed the ball to Cassie, catching her off guard. For some reason she'd expected Emily to kick it down the field. She hesitated a moment too long, and the other team barreled in and took the ball from her.

"Go get it, Cassie!" Emily shouted, already racing after it.

Crapola. Cassie spun on her heel and dashed down the field, slowing when her side began to cramp again. The girls on defense batted the ball back and forth with their feet for a bit before sending it out of reach of the opposing team. It rolled to a stop a mere few feet away from Cassie.

"That's yours, Cassie!" Olivia screamed.

Cassie summoned up a burst of energy and

ran at the ball. She kicked it, feeling a jolt of pleasure when her foot connected. It shot across the grass and suddenly Emily was there, intercepting it and dribbling it toward the opposing goal. The other teammate on offense joined her, and they passed it back and forth, playing off each other. Cassie jogged behind, making an appearance at keeping up but not really.

Emily scored a goal, and Olivia shrieked and cheered. Cassie joined in, smiling and high-fiving her teammates as everyone gathered back behind the starting line. She hadn't done much—kicked the ball once—but nobody really seemed to notice. She let the other teammate take the kick-off, but she felt more prepared this time when the ball came her way.

After fifteen minutes, though, Cassie could no longer pretend to keep up. She lagged behind, walking down the field and clutching her side. Whenever Olivia screamed her name, she put on a burst of speed, only to let it taper off as soon as the ball was out of reach. When Olivia pulled her out so another girl could play, Cassie collapsed next to the red cooler and gulped down a cup of ice water.

"Are you okay, Cassie?" Olivia asked. "You were slowing down out there."

"I'm not used to this heat," Cassie lied. "I just need a break." It had nothing to do with that, and she knew it; but Olivia didn't.

Olivia nodded. "Make sure you drink lots of water, okay? That's what my coach always says. Don't want to get dehydrated."

Cassie bobbed her head and took another sip of water.

Cassie's legs ached by the time they ran back for lunch. Her muscles spasmed even after she sat down, and she was so tired she wasn't even hungry. She poked at her food before stealing up to her room for a rest. They got a two-hour break in the hottest part of the afternoon before hitting the sport hard again. Most of the girls went downstairs to the game room, but Cassie wanted to lay down in cool, air-conditioned silence.

A text from Andrea glowed on her phone screen when Cassie got back to her room. She grabbed the phone, anxious from anything from her best friend, something to make her feel more—valuable.

How is soccer camp? Miss you! Andrea wrote.

Cassie grimaced. How much should she reveal? She replied, *Harder than I expected, but still fun. Miss you like crazy.*

Andrea must've been at her phone, because the response came right away. *Guess what, guess what? I'm so excited, I can't wait to tell you!*

Cassie bounced up and down, grinning, Andrea's excitement contagious even through the phone. *What, what?*

Kitty's parents bought a house here! She'll be at Southwest Junior High with us next year!

Cassie's smile faded, and a rock settled in the back of her throat. Kitty would live here? She'd go to their junior high next year? Cassie swallowed hard. This was not good news. But

Andrea wanted it to be, so . . . *Wow, how exciting! I know you're so glad!*

And that was all she could say. Cassie couldn't pretend to be happy about Kitty moving in, not when she felt insecure and threatened. She closed the phone and slipped it under her pillow, then stretched out on her bed and closed her eyes.

Chapter Three
Cassie the Fat Girl

After three days of camp, Cassie had to admit she could see definite improvements in her passing and blocking. But the running wasn't coming any easier. Though she didn't lose the other campmates again, she still ran at the back of the pack.

Gretchen usually ran with her. Gretchen was a short, heavy-set girl going into ninth grade who liked to be goalie.

"So I don't have to run," she told Cassie on the second day. "That's why I play goalie."

"That's why I play defense," Cassie said, her heart warming to the other girl.

That was yesterday. Today as they jogged along, Gretchen said, "Your sister Emily is doing really well."

"Yeah," Cassie said, straining to keep her feet moving forward. "She's good at everything." It was after lunch, and the afternoon sun beat down on her dark hair, making her head pound.

"Are you two really sisters? You look nothing alike."

"Everyone says that," Cassie said. Sweat beaded along her forehead. "But we're sisters." Both girls had long hair, but that was where the similarities ended. Cassie's was straight and dark brown, almost black, while Emily's was a golden brown with a bit of a wave to it. Cassie's skin sucked up the rays of the sun, turning a nice olive in summer time, while Emily's fair skin had a tendency to burn. They both had brown eyes, though Cassie's were dark as night and Emily's the color of honey.

"Same parents?"

"Yep." She was down to one-word answers. It was all she could manage between panting breaths.

Gretchen fell silent as they rounded the corner to the fields. Then she said, "Some people say running is hard for me because I'm fat."

Cassie turned to study the other girl. While it was true that Gretchen was bigger boned and perhaps heavier set, Cassie would never have called her fat. "No, you're not."

Gretchen smiled at her. "I love your attitude. Us bigger girls have to stick together, right?"

Us bigger girls. Cassie just stared at her.

From the front of the pack, Carol turned around and shouted, "Hurry up, ladies!"

"Razorbacks," Gretchen and Cassie murmured dully.

They caught up to the other girls, and Rishika claimed Gretchen for their team. As Gretchen jogged toward the goal, Cassie tried to make sense of her words. Gretchen considered herself fat. Did she lump Cassie into that same category?

Cassie glanced down at her stomach, bumping out over the rim of her elastic shorts.

Was she fat?

"Cassie," Laine called, "we need you over here!"

She shook off her ponderings and started toward Laine, totally lacking the strength to run anymore. "I call defense."

Gretchen's words ran through Cassie's mind the whole time they scrimmaged. She played her hardest, telling herself to keep running even when she wanted to stop. She threw herself in the ball's path when it came at her, even when she wanted to cringe and duck aside. But ten minutes into it, after she came to a stop on the field and doubled over, hands on her knees and gasping for breath, Laine pulled her out.

"I'm worried you'll get heat exhaustion," Laine said, her pretty features creased with concern. "Your face is so red. Sit down and cool off a bit."

Cassie could only nod and flop onto the grass beside the water cooler. The heat lifted from her face in waves, and she fanned herself. "No one else is getting overheated," she complained when she caught her breath.

Laine turned from where she cheered and coached on the sidelines. "Everyone's different, Cassie. Some people are more built for running."

The words struck a sore spot for Cassie, reminding her of what Gretchen had said. "Are you saying my body's not fit for running?"

Laine just looked at her. Then she shrugged. "I'm sure you can work up to it." Then she went back to watching the team.

Tears stung Cassie's eyes, and she blinked them back. She was fat! How had that happened? When? Why was she just now noticing?

She didn't say anything after practice as she and Gretchen lagged at the back. She urged her legs to lift higher, her feet to pound faster, but no matter what she did, she couldn't seem to change her pace.

The campers entered the dormitory as one and then dispersed, heading to their rooms to change clothes or the bathroom to shower.

Cassie lingered in the shower stall, hoping everyone would have gone to dinner by the time she came out. She didn't want to eat. But as soon as she'd slipped into her clean clothes, her stomach growled, cruelly mocking her.

The door to the communal showers opened, and Emily came in, her room key swinging from the lanyard around her neck. "Cassie? Aren't you coming to dinner?"

"Yes," Cassie said with a sigh, wishing she didn't have to eat.

Emily fell into step beside her as they headed downstairs to the cafeteria. "Everyone's almost done. I wondered where you were."

"I didn't want to eat with everyone else."

"Why?"

Cassie shrugged.

They took the stairs to the cafeteria. Cassie counted each step, hoping they were making her thinner. *One, two, three, four . . .*

Just as Emily had said, most of the campers had already eaten.

"Did you eat?" Cassie asked, looking

around at the vacant tables.

Emily shook her head. "No. I was waiting for you."

"Thanks."

The two girls started down the buffet line as the cafeteria emptied. Cassie considered the pasta, the cheesy broccoli, the meat in tomato sauce, the garlic bread. Were these foods good for her? She opted for a small spoonful of pasta and the cheesy broccoli.

"What's wrong?" Emily asked as they sat down. "You're quiet."

She didn't really know what to say. Cassie picked at her broccoli and sighed. "I'm not doing as well as I hoped I'd be."

"Yes, you are!" Emily exclaimed. "You're improving so much!"

Hot moisture wicked behind Cassie's eyes, and she widened them, willing herself not to cry. "I still can't even run that well. I'm always at the back with Gretchen."

Emily furrowed her brow. "I thought you liked Gretchen."

"I do!" Cassie said. "But—" She hesitated.

How could she say she didn't want to be like Gretchen? "I think I need to work more on my endurance. I want to be healthier."

"But we're constantly running and exercising," Emily said. "We are being healthier."

Cassie thought about that. "Yeah, I guess you're right."

"I mean, we don't run like this at home," Emily said. She gestured at Cassie's plate. "You're gonna need more food than that to keep up your energy."

Feeling a little better, Cassie nodded. "You're right." She finished her pasta and stood up. "Let's get ice cream!"

After the evening practice, the girls gathered in the common room to watch television and play games. Carol sat in a corner on her phone, there if they needed her but for the most part letting them be. This was the perfect chance for Cassie to curl up with a book. She breathed a sigh of contentment, her shoulders relaxing as she slipped into some much-needed down time.

"What are you doing for the talent show?" one girl asked Tara, Cassie's other roommate.

Cassie's eyes wandered over the rim of her book, curious in spite of herself.

Tara was an older girl with long hair and a slender physique. She took the time each morning to put on make-up, even though Olivia teased her there were no boys to impress around here.

Tara shrugged. "I don't know. I've been working on my footwork. I might do something with that."

"I like that idea!" the other girl said. "We could be partners and work off each other."

"Yeah, that could work," Tara agreed. She turned to Olivia, who sat beside her dealing cards. "What are you going to do?"

"Maybe tell some jokes," Olivia said. "I'm pretty funny." Raising her voice, she hollered across the room, "You're going to sing for us, right, Cassie?"

Cassie's face warmed, and she lifted her book up quickly to hide behind it. After reading, singing was what she most loved to do. But being the center of attention embarrassed her. "I don't know."

"What?" Tara exclaimed. "You sing all day long. In our room, in the shower, while you're reading . . ."

Cassie lowered her book just enough to frown at them. "I do?"

"Well, you hum," Olivia qualified. "Practically the same thing."

"Are you a good singer?" Gretchen asked.

"You should hear her," Olivia said, swinging her eyes around to the group. She spoke louder, aware that everyone watched her. "She can sing opera."

"Sing something for us, Cassie!" someone shouted.

"Not now," Tara said, tossing her ponytail behind her shoulders. "Wait until the talent show tomorrow night."

"So you'll sing?" Olivia picked up the deck of cards in front of her and shuffled them.

Cassie nodded. "Yeah. I'll sing." Which meant between now and tomorrow night, she needed to figure out what to sing.

All during practice on Thursday, Cassie tried to figure out what song she'd sing. She wasn't very good at pop music and couldn't remember the words to any song in its entirety. The ball bounced off her several time before she decided it wasn't the time to worry about the talent show. But truthfully, the thought of singing excited her way more than soccer did.

Just before dinner, it came to her: a song she'd learned at Girls Camp last year.

There was no evening practice because of the talent show. Instead, the girls cleaned up and put on costumes and make-up.

Cassie didn't have a costume, and she wasn't allowed to wear make-up. All she had was her Sunday skirt. She put it on and scowled at her reflection. She sucked in her gut, wishing she was skinny and tall like Tara.

"Time for the talent show!" Carol called, walking down the hall and knocking on doors. "Gather in the common room!"

"Here." Olivia grabbed Cassie's arm as she moved toward the door. "You need this." Pulling out a compact of glittery green eyeshadow, she spread it across the backs of Cassie's eyelids. "There. Now you're ready."

Cassie took a deep breath and tried to smile, but her stomach fluttered with nerves.

They sat by Emily and Tara in the common room. Several girls went on stage before Cassie, performing dances and soccer routines and even gymnastics. Cassie tried to enjoy each act, but all she could think about was her upcoming piece. She replayed the words over and over in her head, her fingers tapping out the rhythm on her leg.

Emily walked up the stage and played the piano in the corner, and Cassie's heart went into double-time. It was her turn next. Everyone clapped when Emily finished, and Cassie forced her feet to carry her onto the stage. She took two deep breaths to steady herself, tapped her fingers on her thigh, and started her song.

"Once I dreamt of magic . . ." she sang. Her

voice trembled slightly, but the acoustics in the room bounced the sound waves back to her. The song sounded good, and she stood straighter, more sure of herself. She finished singing and smiled, pleased she hadn't forgotten any of the words.

Everyone clapped.

"But Cassie," Olivia called out, "we wanted opera!"

"Yes," Carol, the camp leader, said from the back of the room. "I was told you can sing opera."

Cassie blinked in surprise. Singing opera was a joke, something she did just for fun.

"Opera! Opera!" Olivia chanted, pumping her fists. The other campers joined in.

"Okay," Cassie said, her heart racing again. They quieted down and looked at her. Clearing her throat, Cassie launched into the familiar song of "Tomorrow," a song everyone knew. Only this time, she sang it as if she were dressed in a viking outfit with lots of fur and a metal helmet and long blond braids. She held her hands out in front of her in dramatic gestures, using her diaphragm to pump out the sound just like her music teacher had taught her.

Carol's face turned beet-red with laughter. She pulled her shirt over her head, her shoulders shaking. The other girls yelled and cheered. When Cassie finished, they all stood up, laughing and clapping for her.

Cassie beamed and made her way back to Emily and Olivia.

"You did superb!" Olivia said, wiping at tears in her eyes. "Oh my. So funny."

The rest of the acts finished up, and Cassie found herself enjoying them, laughing along with the rest of the campers now that her part was over. When it finished, Carol went on stage with a large bag of candy in her hands.

"Girls, that was a lot of fun!" she said, and her words were met with more cheers. "I've laughed till I've cried, and we've all been highly entertained. But one act shone out above the rest. Thus it is with great pleasure that I pronounce the best act of the night. Cassie Jones!"

"Cassie, that's you!" Olivia shrieked. Emily shoved her in the arm, and Cassie pulled herself to her feet. She climbed on the stage and accepted her bag of candy.

"Can we get one more song, Cassie?" Carol said. "One more opera?"

Crapola. She hadn't prepared anything. The campers fell silent, and while they stared at her, Cassie searched her brain. Only one song came to mind, and before she could over think it, she blurted out, in her best operatic soprano, "Happy birthday to you. Happy birthday to you." The rest of the words, though she kept singing, were completely lost in the raucous shouting and hooting erupting from her fellow campers. They didn't stop even after Cassie sat down, and it took Carol a few minutes to calm everyone again.

"Tomorrow is our big game," she said. "After breakfast, we'll all meet at the fields and break into teams. Your parents will be arriving to watch the final play off. This will be your chance to show your skills. With that in mind, even though it's our last night, don't stay up too late! Good night, ladies!"

"Razorbacks!" the girls chorused.

Chapter Four
Final Game

Cassie woke up in the morning with her heart a flutter, and it took her a moment to remember the source of the anxiety. Then she sat up in her bed with a little gasp. Today was the big game day!

"Good morning," Tara said as she shoved something into her suitcase. A quick scan of her bed showed she'd already packed. She also wore her soccer clothes, complete with cleats and shinguards. "Ready for the big game?"

Cassie's heartbeat quickened. Her whole family would be out on the bleachers today, waiting to see how much she'd improved during this camp. "I guess." She rubbed the skin between her eyebrows and then pushed out of bed.

Olivia yawned loudly and stretched her arms. "Morning, ladies!"

"Razorbacks!" Tara crowed.

"Razorbacks," Emily mumbled, still tucked in her blankets on the bed.

Olivia grabbed up her soccer things. "Hurry! We'll have to skip breakfast if we don't eat now!"

Tara went down by herself, but Olivia waited while Emily and Cassie threw on their soccer gear.

"Do you think we'll be on the same team?" Emily asked as they trooped down the stairs together.

"Let's hope so," Olivia said, jumping the last two steps to the floor. "We'll want Cassie's mad defense skills."

Cassie's face warmed with pride as Olivia walked away, and Emily elbowed her.

"See?" she said. "You have improved."

Cassie powered up with eggs and sausage and a piece of toast for good measure. She avoided the pancakes and syrup, certain those foods would only slow her down. Carol entered the cafeteria and clapped her hands, quieting them.

"All right, ladies!" she shouted.

"Razorbacks!" came the expected response.

Carol grinned. "Today's the day to see what you're made of! We've pushed you all week. You've increased your endurance and honed your skills. Let me tell you that your families are on their way now, loading up the bleachers. When we leave this building and run out on that field, you are no longer campers but soccer players! Finish up your food and line up. I want to see what you can do!"

Chairs scraped back from tables as several of the girls jumped up and dumped their plates in the wash bin. Cassie's stomach did a little flip, and she regretted the eggs and sausage she'd eaten. "I think I'm going to be sick," she said, pushing her tray away.

"Then stop eating." Olivia stood as well, grabbing her long curly hair and forcing it back into a ponytail. "Let's play some ball!"

"Come on," Emily said.

Still Cassie lingered. "What if I'm tired by the time we run onto the field? What if I don't have any energy for playing after that?"

Emily looked toward the lobby, where the other campers were gathering, and tapped her foot against the ground. "Let's just go. We'll see what happens."

Emily was right. Cassie cleaned her plate, putting the food in the trash before letting the plate fall into the soapy water. "All right. I'm ready."

They jogged out of the dormitory as one unit, but it wasn't long before Cassie found herself falling behind. Gretchen fell in beside her, matching her pace with a smile.

"Gretchen," Cassie said, panting and trying to ignore the cramping in her side, "I don't want to be the last one on the field today. Do you think we could run a little faster?"

Gretchen pulled the edge of her shirt up and mopped her brow. "You can. I'm good here."

Cassie hesitated. A part of her really didn't

want to leave her friend behind, but an even bigger part of her didn't want to be the last one on the field. "Okay. I'll see you there." With that, she put on a burst of speed. Her lungs ached as she forced herself to take deep breaths and catch up with the other girls.

Nobody spoke as they ran, and Cassie realized that even though they made it look easy, running was hard on all of them. The morning sun beat down on them. As they rounded the corner onto the fields, a loud cheer broke out. Cassie's eyes swept upward to the bleachers, and she saw people in shorts and brightly colored shirts standing there, clapping their hands and waving.

Carol blew her whistle, and Cassie focused on finishing their jog around the field. They came to a stop on the white line in front of the bleachers, and finally the girls had the chance to yell and wave back to their parents. Cassie found her family. Annette and Scott stood on the seats, enthusiastically bouncing up and down. Her mom and dad stood close by, beaming down at them. Cassie waved and stood up straighter. This was her chance to make them proud. She'd show them what she'd learned.

Carol pulled them all back in a huddle. She numbered them off and assigned placements. "Cassie, team two, defense. But I want you to sit out first quarter." She handed her a blue vest, and Cassie slipped it on. "Emily, team one, offense." Carol handed Emily the yellow vest.

Cassie stole a quick glance at her sister, but Emily's eyes were honed on Carol, her expression serious. Cassie frowned. She hadn't planned on playing against her sister. How would her parents know who to cheer for?

Assignments made, Carol blew the whistle again, and the girls scattered. Cassie made her way to the sidelines and sat down on the grass, watching as Emily got into position behind the starting line. Olivia stood next to her, playing offense alongside her. Cassie turned to her own teammates. Tara was on defense, and Gretchen was in goal.

The other girls sitting out the first quarter settled in behind Cassie. They talked and whispered, but Cassie made no effort to scoot back and join them. Instead, she picked a blade of grass and shredded it while she watched the teams face off. Should she root for her sister, or her own team?

The whistle blew, Olivia passed the ball to Emily, and Emily took off down the field. Cassie straightened up as Tara ran to intercept. Emily's foot-work evaded her, and soon she was past Tara, streaming toward the goal.

"Come on!" Cassie shouted, wishing she were out there. She'd stop her sister.

Gretchen ran out of the goalie box and launched herself at Emily, but Emily passed the ball to Olivia. Before Gretchen could pivot, Olivia shot the ball over her head and into the goal.

Cassie sighed and stood up. "Carol," she shouted as the two teams lined up again.

Carol glanced toward her, squinting a little and shielding her eyes.

"Put me in," Cassie said. "I want to play."

"You'll go in soon," Carol said. Then she spun around and returned her attention to the field.

Cassie sat down again. She tapped her feet on the grass, watching anxiously as the teams started up. The blue team had the ball this time, and they quickly swept it past the offense and took it downfield. But as soon as they hit the defensive line, they met resistance. The yellow team blocked their passes and pushed them backward, until suddenly Olivia was there, taking the ball away from the blue team and driving it back to the yellow team.

Cassie groaned and tugged at her hair. Olivia and Emily played off each other like choreographed dancers, occasionally passing the ball to Nikki, who was also playing offense. Cassie stood up and paced in agitation. Once again, they approached the goal. The other defender ran out and met them, but Olivia quickly sidestepped her. They were going to score again!

Tara swooped in, blocking Olivia's pass. She kicked the ball high overhead, sending it into the safe zone on the other side of the field. Cassie exhaled in relief.

"Cassie!" Carol shouted, jogging over. "You're up. Defense. Tara! Come sit out!"

Cassie and Tara exchanged high-fives as they passed each other, but Cassie wished the other girl was staying on the field. She didn't really know Rachel, the other defender, and she didn't seem to be as good a player as Tara. They nodded at each other and then waited midfield.

Cassie steeled herself as the yellow team seized the ball and worked it back toward her. She rocked on the heels of her feet, waiting for the right moment to run out and intercept. This time it was Olivia and Nikki coming her way. Cassie waited—and waited—and now! She shot forward, getting between the two girls. Nikki had the ball and tried to outmaneuver her, but Cassie closed in, placing her feet next to Nikki's and stealing touches to the ball. Olivia and Emily drew near, and Cassie kicked the ball behind her, hoping Rachel would be there.

She was. In the open, with no one else around, Rachel knocked the ball away from their goal.

"Here!" someone on offense shouted, and Rachel passed it upfield.

Cheers from the stands erupted, and Cassie's shoulders relaxed a bit as the blue strikers ran the ball toward the other goal. And then she found herself holding her breath as they got closer and closer to the goal. The blue team kicked, the yellow goalie ran out to meet it, and then—

"We scored!" Rachel shouted.

Cassie threw her hands in the air and did a happy dance with her. Now they were tied, one-to-one. And she'd actually played. She'd done something valuable. Her heart swelled, and she readied herself for the next round.

The game finished five to four, with the yellow team winning. Even though Cassie's team lost, she felt proud of their efforts. She'd played two straight quarters, taking a break at half-time but quickly coming back in for the third quarter. And she'd been a contributor, running and fighting for the ball instead of slugging down the field.

When the game ended, Carol gave a brief speech about how much they'd improved. Then she handed each girl a medal and sent them out to meet their parents.

"Great job, girls!" Mrs. Jones said, opening her arms to hug Cassie and Emily.

"We're sweaty," Cassie said, sidestepping the hug and sitting down next to Scott and Annette instead.

"Good hustle out there," Mr. Jones said. "Looks like you girls really learned some soccer skills."

Cassie nodded and took a sip of her water bottle. She had learned, and she was proud of how she'd played. But it wasn't quite enough. She needed to work on more than just her physical endurance. Her eyes slipped down to the bulge beneath her red shirt, hanging out over the elastic band of her shorts.

"Do you like your soccer shorts?" Mr. Jones

asked.

"Yeah!" Cassie said, her eyes lighting up as she remembered what her mother had told them. "They're from your new soccer store, right?"

"It's not open yet." He grinned, a child-like excitement on his face that Cassie rarely saw. "The grand opening's right before school starts. I'll teach you how to do the register before then."

"I can't wait!" Cassie squealed.

"And me too?" Emily asked.

"When you're older," he said, tugging her ponytail.

"But first you have church camp," Mrs. Jones said. "Then you can worry about working for your dad."

Cassie held in a groan. She was not looking forward to church camp, with the snobby clique of girls who ignored her every Wednesday and Sunday. She'd prefer to do another week of grueling soccer camp over that.

Chapter Five
Wedding

Andrea texted Cassie on Sunday.

Ms. Timber's wedding is next Saturday. Want to spend the night and ride together?

Cassie's eyes widened. With soccer camp going on, she'd completely forgotten about their sixth grade teacher's upcoming wedding. She quickly texted back. *I'll ask my mom, but plan on it! What fun!*

Mrs. Jones said yes, and Friday night she dropped Cassie off at Andrea's house.

"Hi!" Andrea exclaimed, hugging her tight and rocking back and forth as if they hadn't seen each other in years. "I missed you! What are you, like a star soccer player now?"

"Hardly," Cassie said with a laugh. She followed Andrea to her room and dropped her overnight bag on the bed. "It was so much fun, but I just don't think I'm that good at it. I think—" Cassie hesitated to say these words out loud. The idea had been rolling around in her head for a few weeks now, but to say it out loud was a kind of commitment. She plunged onward. "I think I need to go on a diet."

Andrea blinked at her. "Really?" she said, her voice hushed. "To get skinny?"

Cassie nodded, placing her hands around her waist and squeezing the excess skin there. "I just feel like if I were a bit thinner, things like running would be easier."

"I think you look fine," Andrea said.

Cassie smiled at her. "Thanks. But I'm going to. My clothes will fit a bit better too, I think."

"What kind of diet?"

Cassie shrugged. She hadn't thought that far. "I don't know. Just eat less, I guess."

Andrea frowned and looked down at herself. "Do I need to go on a diet?"

Cassie appraised her best friend. She'd never thought Andrea needed to change anything at all. "I don't think so."

"I don't think you need to, either."

She didn't want to talk about it anymore. "So tell me about Kitty." She put on a smile and tried to look excited. "What's going on?"

Andrea perked right up. "Her family bought a house not too far from here. She's planning on going to Southwest with us!"

"Wow," Cassie said, still smiling.

"Yes! I can't wait until orientation. Maybe we'll have classes together."

"Maybe," Cassie echoed. She tried to shrug off her insecurities. The friendship she and Andrea had was strong enough to allow other good friends. As long as Cassie remained Andrea's best friend.

"I bought this heart paper." Andrea opened a drawer and pulled out thick card stock, white with red hearts on it. "I thought it might be nice for us to make a card for Ms. Timber."

"That's a great idea," Cassie said, happy for

the subject change.

Andrea folded the card stock in half and wrote across the top,

To Ms. Timber. On your lucky day.

"What's Ms. Timber's new last name going to be?" Cassie asked.

"Something really weird. Let me find the invitation." Andrea left the room, and Cassie took the moment to survey it. She loved Andrea's room, with the full bed covered in a pink bedspread, to the closet with the sliding door, always overflowing with cute skirts and tops. A bookshelf next to the bed held a few books, but mostly old toys and cute knick-knacks. The white vanity pressed against the opposite wall, full of drawers and cubbies and a jewelry box on top. Countless hours Cassie had sat in that chair, staring at her reflection while Andrea curled her hair or did her make-up. Cassie sat there now, pushing her glasses up on her nose and staring at herself. Her round face, tanned from soccer camp and with a sprinkling of freckles across her nose, peered back at her. A plastic blue headband held back her long dark hair. What did other people see when they looked at her?

Andrea returned with the invitation and set it in front of Cassie. "Snodgrass." She giggled. "I knew it was something weird."

Cassie picked it up. From Ms. Timber to Ms. Snodgrass. "It's not such a bad name," she said. "Not if it's the man you love."

"Oh, of course." Andrea leaned in close, pressing her cheek against Cassie's and uttering a sigh as she stared at their reflections. "But of course, your last name will be Hansen." She batted her eyes and puckered her lips.

Heat crept up Cassie's cheeks, rushing all the way to her hairline. "Miles and I are just friends," she said. "Though it is a nice last name," she added with a small smile.

Andrea burst out laughing and settled back on the bed. "Cassandra Hansen! I love it."

Cassie picked up a nail file and lowered her eyes to hide how much the sound of that pleased her. Maybe if she were skinnier, Miles would like her back.

Cassie and Andrea put on dressy clothes the next morning. Cassie had brought her black leather pin skirt, the one her mom said was too short to be decent. It just barely hit the tops of her knees. She paired it with a red blouse and imagined she looked grown up and sophisticated. However, a glance in the mirror said otherwise. The skirt pinched a little too tightly around the waist, making the blouse bunch up and wrinkle. Cassie tugged up and down and finally got the skirt in a place where it didn't pinch, but now it was two inches above her knee.

Andrea came into the room from the bathroom, already dressed in a sleeveless floral dress. "Wow, you look sexy," she said, eyeing Cassie's skirt.

"It's not supposed to be this high," Cassie admitted. "My mom would kill me."

"Good thing your mom won't be there," Andrea said. She opened her jewelry box and pulled out a gold chain. "Miles will love it."

Would he? Cassie frowned at her reflection. All she could see was a fat girl.

She forgot her concerns when Mrs. Wall dropped the two girls off at the chapel. They found most of their classmates in the back and crowded into the pews next to them, whispering and gossiping excitedly. A quick survey of her classmates showed Miles wasn't among them. The groom stood at the front of the chapel in front of beautiful stained glass windows, a handsome man with dark blond hair and a black tux. He faced the aisle with an air of expectancy. Cassie craned her neck, trying to peer past her classmates and get a glimpse of the bride.

The organ music started, and everyone stood up. Cassie did as well. She'd never been to a wedding and didn't really know what was going on, but she wasn't about to sit when no one else was.

A moment later, Ms. Timber appeared. Her short dark hair had been piled on top of her head and trapped with a small tiara. Ringlets framed her face and escaped down the nape of her neck. Cassie took in a sharp breath at the sight of the dress. The fluffy, billowing skirt emphasized Ms. Timber's slender waist, and pink embroidery and pink pearls decorated the satiny fabric.

Beautiful, Cassie thought.

The man's face broke into a smile, and Ms. Timber beamed back at him, radiant in her happiness. Cassie closed her eyes, lost in a moment of euphoria. Would she someday feel such happiness as she walked down the aisle to marry a man who loved her as much as this man loved Ms. Timber? She opened her eyes and leaned forward, breathless with hope.

The vows passed by in a blur, and then they kissed. The whole ceremony was incredibly romantic, and Cassie clasped her hands together, trembling with anticipation. If only, if only, if only. Surely this would be her one day.

The guests filed out of the chapel and into a reception room, where the new Mr. and Mrs. Snodgrass cut their cake. As soon as that was done, everyone entered a line at the buffet. Cassie took a quick inventory of the available food. Meatballs in sauce, little pieces of cheese, bread slices, bacon-wrapped dates. It all looked exquisite and so not good for her.

She poured herself a cup of water and sat down, averting her eyes from the food line. Her mouth watered, and she wanted very much to fill a plate with her classmates.

"Aren't you going to eat, Cassie?" Andrea asked, sitting down across from her.

The aromas of cooked meats and melted cheese wafted toward her, and Cassie nearly caved. And then she spotted someone. Lingering against the wall, back straight and not talking to anyone, was Betsy Walker.

Betsy. Cassie hadn't seen her since child services took Betsy away from her parents last spring and placed her in a house with her aunt in Mountain Home.

"Maybe later," she said, pushing away from the table and heading toward her.

Before Betsy left, she had been a giggly girl who sat by Cassie on the bus every day, full of life and laughter and comfort. She'd come to Cassie's birthday when no one else had. She'd stayed by Cassie's side after the death of her beloved dog. And she'd cried out her fears to Cassie the one time her social worker arranged a visit between them.

None of those emotions showed on her face now. Her expression was closed and drawn, her eyes blank and hooded. She stood stiff, a drink in her hand, her lips in a rigid line. Her blond hair hung a little longer, flipping out just below her shoulder blades.

"Betsy?" Cassie said, suddenly uncertain.

Betsy's eyes turned toward her. "Cassie," she said, but she didn't smile. She still stood as stiff and rigid as before.

Cassie paused beside the wall. "How are you?" she asked. "Do you still live in Mountain Home?"

Betsy nodded and took a sip of her punch. "My aunt insisted I come to this."

"Oh." Cassie hesitated, then held an arm out to indicate her classmates. "But aren't you glad you did? Aren't you happy to see all your friends?"

Betsy shrugged. "These people aren't my friends."

"But I'm your friend," Cassie said.

Betsy finally looked at her, and some of her hard façade cracked beneath a brief smile. "Yes. You're my friend."

Cassie relaxed and slid closer, leaning against the wall beside her. "Are things going all right?"

Betsy didn't reply, and Cassie supposed that was answer enough. They stood there in silence, and then Cassie reached over and squeezed Betsy's hand.

"I miss you," she said.

Tears sprang to Betsy's eyes, and her lips moved, murmuring something. Cassie didn't catch the words.

"I've got to go," Betsy said. She turned and wrapped her arms around Cassie, squeezing her tight. "Thank you." She let go and slipped out the door, and Cassie turned to watch. Her own eyes burned, and she blinked back the moisture that gathered there.

"So disappointing," Andrea said as Mrs. Wall drove them home after the wedding. "Miles wasn't there."

"I know," Cassie said. But maybe that was a good thing. She didn't like how she looked in this skirt.

"How was the ceremony?" Mrs. Wall asked.

"Beautiful," Cassie said, just as Andrea said, "Dreamy."

The girls looked at each other and giggled.

"Some day that will be us," Andrea said.

"To be loved like that," Cassie sighed.

"Her dress was exquisite," Andrea said.

"The pink!" Cassie exclaimed. "I could barely breathe!"

"I know," Andrea agreed. She grabbed Cassie's hands and squeezed them. "I want a dress just like hers."

"With a sparkling tiara."

"And my hair done in soft curls."

"Piled on top of my head."

They both sighed loudly, relishing in their delicious fantasies.

"All right, girls," Mrs. Wall chuckled, pulling the car into the driveway. "At least we have it set in stone that you both want beautiful weddings one day. Now let's settle back into reality. You're only twelve with many years ahead of you. Don't forget to enjoy life right now."

"We won't," Andrea said.

"Yeah," Cassie agreed. Besides, she wasn't ready to get married yet. There were too many things she needed to do first.

"Do you want to come over again next week?" Andrea asked as Cassie changed out of the tight black skirt and into the jeans she'd worn the day before.

"I wish," Cassie said with an unhappy sigh. "I have church camp."

"Won't that be fun?"

"No." Cassie shook her head. "I don't like any of the other girls. And they don't like me."

"You could skip it," Andrea suggested.

"Would love to, but my mom won't let me."

A car honked outside, and Cassie

shouldered her overnight bag. "That's my mom. I'll see you later."

Andrea hugged her. "Text me."

"Oh." That reminded Cassie of another reason she wasn't excited about church camp. "No electronics. I won't be able to talk to you until next Saturday."

Andrea looked disappointed, but she nodded. "That's all right. I'll see what Kitty's doing."

Cassie gritted her teeth. Like salt to the wound. "Glad you'll have someone to hang out with," she said instead. Then she turned and headed for the front door.

Episode 1: Growing Girl

Available Now!

Episode 2: Lost in School

The path meandered along a small creek, several giant rocks causing small waterfalls to form as the stream tumbled down the hillside. The air grew hotter and more stifling, and sweat made Cassie's glasses slide down her nose. She stopped several times as they hiked upward, pressing her hand to her chest and trying to catch her breath. She could see the rest of the campers in a little pool at the top, some of them stepping into the water and splashing while others took pictures.

"That wasn't too bad at all," Elise said when they reached the top. The few remaining girls came up the hill behind them. Elise pulled out her phone and used the camera function to take a panorama shot of the woods and waterfall.

"Yeah, it was fun," Tesia agreed.

"Yeah," Cassie echoed, though her chest felt tight and swollen. Her head pounded like a drummer had taken up residence. One hand massaged the area just above her heart, and the other pressed against her scalp.

"Are you okay?" Elise asked, looking up from the pictures.

"Just hot," Cassie said.

"Drink more water." Tesia uncapped the canteen and handed it to her.

Cassie took a drink, and a little shudder ran through her. "I'm fine," she said. She sat down on a rock and took her shoes off, letting her feet rest in the water. Tesia and Elise started jumping along the rocks, leaning over to peer at the water tumbling down the hill.

"Ah!" Elise shrieked when Tesia gave her a playful shove. She turned around and pushed Tesia backwards into the shallow creek. Tesia landed on her bum, laughing.

"Everyone out of the water!" Sister Mecham marched through them, a frown etched on her face. "I said we'd meet up here, not go swimming up here." She looked at the older girls as if they were responsible. They climbed out, and the younger girls followed.

"Good job on your stations," she said, facing them all. "When we get back to the campsite, get your camp books and have your leaders sign off your requirements."

Cassie put her shoes back on and stood up. Her feet felt good, but the rest of her body seemed to be emanating heat. She poured some water from her canteen into her hands and splashed it on her face.

"That was so fun," Elise said, joining her. Tesia came as well, and the three of them started down the hillside behind the other campers.

"You're quiet, Cassie," Elise commented.

Cassie didn't answer. It took all her concentration to put each foot in front of her and not stumble.

Tesia touched her arm. "Do you need to rest?"

Cassie hesitated and then came to a stop. "Yes. Let's rest just for a minute."

The three girls stood in silence, watching the

campers in front of them move down the hill. Cassie took several deep breaths and another sip of her water.

"Okay," she exhaled. "We can go again."

They started forward, and then Cassie's head grew so hot she thought it might explode. She sank down to the ground and sat on the compacted dirt. Tesia and Elise crouched next to her, exchanging worried looks.

"Are you okay?" Elise asked.

Cassie closed her eyes and laid her head back.

"Let's just hurry up and get her back to camp," Tesia said, her voice anxious.

"Come on, Cassie." Elise picked her up under her arms. "We have to keep moving."

Cassie opened her eyes and tried to help, but she couldn't seem to get her legs under her.

"At least we learned how to do the dead man's carry," Tesia joked.

"Humph," Elise grunted.

Tesia took another arm, and together they

dragged Cassie over the rocks and sticks bumping out of the ground.

"I don't remember the way back to camp," Tesia panted.

"It's down the hill," Elise said. "Just keep going."

Cassie felt the moment they left the worn path beside the creek and entered the heavy underbrush of the forest. Bushes snagged her hair and plants caught themselves in her clothes.

"How far is it?" Tesia gasped.

"I can't keep going like this," Elise moaned.

"I'm sorry," Cassie murmured, opening her eyes to squint at them. Sunlight dappled their clothing as it attempted to pierce the thick foliage above.

"Don't you even worry," Elise said, stroking her arm. She turned to Tesia. "I have to go to camp. I have to get help."

Tesia nodded. "We'll wait right here. Be careful."

"Give her water." Elise unhooked her own canteen and handed it to Tesia. "Keep her cool." With that, she turned around and darted off, ducking and dodging branches as she ran through the plant life.

About the Author

Tamara Hart Heiner is a mom, wife, baker, editor, and author. She currently lives in Arkansas with her husband, four children, a cat, a rabbit, a dog, and a fish. She would love to add a macaw and a sugar glider to the family. She's the author of several young adult suspense series (*Perilous, Goddess of Fate, Kellam High*) the *Cassandra Jones* saga, and a nonfiction book about the Joplin Tornado, *Tornado Warning.*

Connect with Tamara online!
Twitter: https://twitter.com/tamaraheiner
Facebook:
https://www.facebook.com/author.tamara.heiner
blog:
http://www.tamarahartheiner/blogspot.com
website: http://www.tamarahartheiner.com
Thank you for reading!